THIS BOOK BELONGS TO

EMAIL:

ADDRESS:

CONTACT:

PHONE:

START DATE	END DATE

MO TU WE TH FR SA SU
☐   ☐   ☐   ☐   ☐   ☐   ☐

DATE: /   /

PROJECT:

FOREMAN:

WEATHER

F°_____ C°_____   _____ AM   _____ PM

HOURS DUE TO
BAD WEATHER

ISSUED AND DELAYS

NOTE: ____

COMPLETION DATE	DAYS AHEAD OF SCHEDULE	DAYS BEHIND SCHEDULE

SAFETY AND INCIDENTS

SAFETY ISSUES THAT NEED TO BE ADDRESSED	ACCIDENTS / INCIDENTS / STEPS NEEDED TO RESOLVE

SUMMARY OF THE WORK DONE TODAY

IMPORTANT NOTES

NAME	SIGNATURE

TODAY LABOR

INITIALS	TRADE	START	FINISH	PAID HOURS	OVERTIME	COMPANY
☐ EMPLOYEE ☐ CONTRUCTOR		AM	PM			
☐ EMPLOYEE ☐ CONTRUCTOR		AM	PM			
☐ EMPLOYEE ☐ CONTRUCTOR		AM	PM			
☐ EMPLOYEE ☐ CONTRUCTOR		AM	PM			
☐ EMPLOYEE ☐ CONTRUCTOR		AM	PM			
☐ EMPLOYEE ☐ CONTRUCTOR		AM	PM			
☐ EMPLOYEE ☐ CONTRUCTOR		AM	PM			
☐ EMPLOYEE ☐ CONTRUCTOR		AM	PM			

EQUIPMENT ON SITE	NO. OF UNITE	WORKING YES / NO

HIRED EQUIPMENT	NO. OF UNITE	EQUIPMENT RENTED	FROM	RATE

NAME: _______________________   SIGNATURE: _______________________

MO TU WE TH FR SA SU
☐   ☐   ☐   ☐   ☐   ☐   ☐

DATE: /   /

PROJECT:

FOREMAN:

WEATHER   F°_____ C°_____   _____ AM   _____ PM

HOURS DUE TO BAD WEATHER

ISSUED AND DELAYS

NOTE: _______________________________

COMPLETION DATE	DAYS AHEAD OF SCHEDULE	DAYS BEHIND SCHEDULE

SAFETY AND INCIDENTS

SAFETY ISSUES THAT NEED TO BE ADDRESSED	ACCIDENTS / INCIDENTS / STEPS NEEDED TO RESOLVE

SUMMARY OF THE WORK DONE TODAY

IMPORTANT NOTES

NAME	SIGNATURE

INITIALS	TRADE	START	FINISH	PAID HOURS	OVERTIME	COMPANY
☐ EMPLOYEE ☐ CONTRUCTOR		AM	PM			
☐ EMPLOYEE ☐ CONTRUCTOR		AM	PM			
☐ EMPLOYEE ☐ CONTRUCTOR		AM	PM			
☐ EMPLOYEE ☐ CONTRUCTOR		AM	PM			
☐ EMPLOYEE ☐ CONTRUCTOR		AM	PM			
☐ EMPLOYEE ☐ CONTRUCTOR		AM	PM			
☐ EMPLOYEE ☐ CONTRUCTOR		AM	PM			
☐ EMPLOYEE ☐ CONTRUCTOR		AM	PM			

EQUIPMENT ON SITE	NO. OF UNITE	WORKING YES / NO

HIRED EQUIPMENT	NO. OF UNITE	EQUIPMENT RENTED	FROM	RATE

NAME: _______________________   SIGNATURE: _______________________

MO   TU   WE   TH   FR   SA   SU
☐   ☐   ☐   ☐   ☐   ☐   ☐

DATE: /   /

PROJECT:

FOREMAN:

WEATHER   F°_____ C°_____   _____ AM   _____ PM

HOURS DUE TO BAD WEATHER	ISSUED AND DELAYS

NOTE: ____

COMPLETION DATE	DAYS AHEAD OF SCHEDULE	DAYS BEHIND SCHEDULE

SAFETY AND INCIDENTS

SAFETY ISSUES THAT NEED TO BE ADDRESSED	ACCIDENTS / INCIDENTS / STEPS NEEDED TO RESOLVE

SUMMARY OF THE WORK DONE TODAY

IMPORTANT NOTES

NAME	SIGNATURE

TODAY LABOR

INITIALS	TRADE	START	FINISH	PAID HOURS	OVERTIME	COMPANY
☐ EMPLOYEE ☐ CONTRUCTOR		AM	PM			
☐ EMPLOYEE ☐ CONTRUCTOR		AM	PM			
☐ EMPLOYEE ☐ CONTRUCTOR		AM	PM			
☐ EMPLOYEE ☐ CONTRUCTOR		AM	PM			
☐ EMPLOYEE ☐ CONTRUCTOR		AM	PM			
☐ EMPLOYEE ☐ CONTRUCTOR		AM	PM			
☐ EMPLOYEE ☐ CONTRUCTOR		AM	PM			
☐ EMPLOYEE ☐ CONTRUCTOR		AM	PM			

EQUIPMENT ON SITE	NO. OF UNITE	WORKING YES / NO

HIRED EQUIPMENT	NO. OF UNITE	EQUIPMENT RENTED	FROM	RATE

NAME: _______________________   SIGNATURE: _______________________

MO TU WE TH FR SA SU
☐   ☐   ☐   ☐   ☐   ☐   ☐

DATE: / /

PROJECT:

FOREMAN:

WEATHER

F°_____ C°_____ _____ AM _____ PM

HOURS DUE TO BAD WEATHER	ISSUED AND DELAYS

NOTE: _______________________

COMPLETION DATE	DAYS AHEAD OF SCHEDULE	DAYS BEHIND SCHEDULE

SAFETY AND INCIDENTS

SAFETY ISSUES THAT NEED TO BE ADDRESSED	ACCIDENTS / INCIDENTS / STEPS NEEDED TO RESOLVE

SUMMARY OF THE WORK DONE TODAY

IMPORTANT NOTES

NAME	SIGNATURE

TODAY LABOR							
INITIALS	TRADE	START	FINISH	PAID HOURS	OVERTIME	COMPANY
☐ EMPLOYEE ☐ CONTRUCTOR		AM	PM			
☐ EMPLOYEE ☐ CONTRUCTOR		AM	PM			
☐ EMPLOYEE ☐ CONTRUCTOR		AM	PM			
☐ EMPLOYEE ☐ CONTRUCTOR		AM	PM			
☐ EMPLOYEE ☐ CONTRUCTOR		AM	PM			
☐ EMPLOYEE ☐ CONTRUCTOR		AM	PM			
☐ EMPLOYEE ☐ CONTRUCTOR		AM	PM			
☐ EMPLOYEE ☐ CONTRUCTOR		AM	PM			

EQUIPMENT ON SITE	NO. OF UNITE	WORKING YES / NO

HIRED EQUIPMENT	NO. OF UNITE	EQUIPMENT RENTED	FROM	RATE

NAME: _______________________   SIGNATURE: _______________________

MO TU WE TH FR SA SU
☐   ☐   ☐   ☐   ☐   ☐   ☐

DATE: / /

PROJECT:

FOREMAN:

WEATHER

F° ____ C° ____   ____ AM   ____ PM

HOURS DUE TO BAD WEATHER

ISSUED AND DELAYS

NOTE:

COMPLETION DATE	DAYS AHEAD OF SCHEDULE	DAYS BEHIND SCHEDULE

SAFETY AND INCIDENTS

SAFETY ISSUES THAT NEED TO BE ADDRESSED	ACCIDENTS / INCIDENTS / STEPS NEEDED TO RESOLVE

SUMMARY OF THE WORK DONE TODAY

IMPORTANT NOTES

NAME	SIGNATURE

TODAY LABOR						
INITIALS	TRADE	START	FINISH	PAID HOURS	OVERTIME	COMPANY
☐ EMPLOYEE ☐ CONTRUCTOR		AM	PM			
☐ EMPLOYEE ☐ CONTRUCTOR		AM	PM			
☐ EMPLOYEE ☐ CONTRUCTOR		AM	PM			
☐ EMPLOYEE ☐ CONTRUCTOR		AM	PM			
☐ EMPLOYEE ☐ CONTRUCTOR		AM	PM			
☐ EMPLOYEE ☐ CONTRUCTOR		AM	PM			
☐ EMPLOYEE ☐ CONTRUCTOR		AM	PM			
☐ EMPLOYEE ☐ CONTRUCTOR		AM	PM			

EQUIPMENT ON SITE	NO. OF UNITE	WORKING YES / NO

HIRED EQUIPMENT	NO. OF UNITE	EQUIPMENT RENTED	FROM	RATE

NAME: _______________________________   SIGNATURE: _______________________________

MO TU WE TH FR SA SU
☐   ☐   ☐   ☐   ☐   ☐   ☐

DATE: /   /

PROJECT:

FOREMAN:

WEATHER

F°_____ C°_____   _____ AM   _____ PM

HOURS DUE TO BAD WEATHER	ISSUED AND DELAYS

NOTE: _______________________________________

COMPLETION DATE	DAYS AHEAD OF SCHEDULE	DAYS BEHIND SCHEDULE

SAFETY AND INCIDENTS

SAFETY ISSUES THAT NEED TO BE ADDRESSED	ACCIDENTS / INCIDENTS / STEPS NEEDED TO RESOLVE

SUMMARY OF THE WORK DONE TODAY

IMPORTANT NOTES

NAME	SIGNATURE

TODAY LABOR

INITIALS	TRADE	START	FINISH	PAID HOURS	OVERTIME	COMPANY
☐ EMPLOYEE ☐ CONTRUCTOR		AM	PM			
☐ EMPLOYEE ☐ CONTRUCTOR		AM	PM			
☐ EMPLOYEE ☐ CONTRUCTOR		AM	PM			
☐ EMPLOYEE ☐ CONTRUCTOR		AM	PM			
☐ EMPLOYEE ☐ CONTRUCTOR		AM	PM			
☐ EMPLOYEE ☐ CONTRUCTOR		AM	PM			
☐ EMPLOYEE ☐ CONTRUCTOR		AM	PM			
☐ EMPLOYEE ☐ CONTRUCTOR		AM	PM			

EQUIPMENT ON SITE	NO. OF UNITE	WORKING YES / NO

HIRED EQUIPMENT	NO. OF UNITE	EQUIPMENT RENTED	FROM	RATE

NAME: _______________   SIGNATURE: _______________

MO TU WE TH FR SA SU
☐   ☐   ☐   ☐   ☐   ☐   ☐

DATE: ___ / ___ / ___

PROJECT:

FOREMAN:

WEATHER

F° _____ C° _____   _____ AM _____ PM

HOURS DUE TO BAD WEATHER	ISSUED AND DELAYS

NOTE: ____

COMPLETION DATE	DAYS AHEAD OF SCHEDULE	DAYS BEHIND SCHEDULE

SAFETY AND INCIDENTS

SAFETY ISSUES THAT NEED TO BE ADDRESSED	ACCIDENTS / INCIDENTS / STEPS NEEDED TO RESOLVE

SUMMARY OF THE WORK DONE TODAY

IMPORTANT NOTES

NAME	SIGNATURE

TODAY LABOR

INITIALS	TRADE	START	FINISH	PAID HOURS	OVERTIME	COMPANY
☐ EMPLOYEE ☐ CONTRUCTOR		AM	PM			
☐ EMPLOYEE ☐ CONTRUCTOR		AM	PM			
☐ EMPLOYEE ☐ CONTRUCTOR		AM	PM			
☐ EMPLOYEE ☐ CONTRUCTOR		AM	PM			
☐ EMPLOYEE ☐ CONTRUCTOR		AM	PM			
☐ EMPLOYEE ☐ CONTRUCTOR		AM	PM			
☐ EMPLOYEE ☐ CONTRUCTOR		AM	PM			
☐ EMPLOYEE ☐ CONTRUCTOR		AM	PM			

EQUIPMENT ON SITE	NO. OF UNITE	WORKING YES / NO

HIRED EQUIPMENT	NO. OF UNITE	EQUIPMENT RENTED	FROM	RATE

NAME: _______________________   SIGNATURE: _______________________

MO   TU   WE   TH   FR   SA   SU
☐   ☐   ☐   ☐   ☐   ☐   ☐

DATE: ___/___/___

PROJECT:

FOREMAN:

WEATHER   F°_____ C°_____   _____ AM   _____ PM

HOURS DUE TO BAD WEATHER	ISSUED AND DELAYS

NOTE: ____

COMPLETION DATE	DAYS AHEAD OF SCHEDULE	DAYS BEHIND SCHEDULE

SAFETY AND INCIDENTS

SAFETY ISSUES THAT NEED TO BE ADDRESSED	ACCIDENTS / INCIDENTS / STEPS NEEDED TO RESOLVE

SUMMARY OF THE WORK DONE TODAY

IMPORTANT NOTES

NAME	SIGNATURE

<table>
<tr><td colspan="7" align="center">TODAY LABOR</td></tr>
<tr><td>INITIALS</td><td>TRADE</td><td>START</td><td>FINISH</td><td>PAID HOURS</td><td>OVERTIME</td><td>COMPANY</td></tr>
<tr><td>☐ EMPLOYEE
☐ CONTRUCTOR</td><td></td><td>AM</td><td>PM</td><td></td><td></td><td></td></tr>
<tr><td>☐ EMPLOYEE
☐ CONTRUCTOR</td><td></td><td>AM</td><td>PM</td><td></td><td></td><td></td></tr>
<tr><td>☐ EMPLOYEE
☐ CONTRUCTOR</td><td></td><td>AM</td><td>PM</td><td></td><td></td><td></td></tr>
<tr><td>☐ EMPLOYEE
☐ CONTRUCTOR</td><td></td><td>AM</td><td>PM</td><td></td><td></td><td></td></tr>
<tr><td>☐ EMPLOYEE
☐ CONTRUCTOR</td><td></td><td>AM</td><td>PM</td><td></td><td></td><td></td></tr>
<tr><td>☐ EMPLOYEE
☐ CONTRUCTOR</td><td></td><td>AM</td><td>PM</td><td></td><td></td><td></td></tr>
<tr><td>☐ EMPLOYEE
☐ CONTRUCTOR</td><td></td><td>AM</td><td>PM</td><td></td><td></td><td></td></tr>
<tr><td>☐ EMPLOYEE
☐ CONTRUCTOR</td><td></td><td>AM</td><td>PM</td><td></td><td></td><td></td></tr>
</table>

EQUIPMENT ON SITE	NO. OF UNITE	WORKING YES / NO

HIRED EQUIPMENT	NO. OF UNITE	EQUIPMENT RENTED	FROM	RATE

NAME: _______________________   SIGNATURE: _______________________

MO TU WE TH FR SA SU
☐   ☐   ☐   ☐   ☐   ☐   ☐

DATE: /   /

PROJECT:

FOREMAN:

WEATHER

F°_____ C°_____   _____ AM   _____ PM

HOURS DUE TO BAD WEATHER	ISSUED AND DELAYS

NOTE: ____

COMPLETION DATE	DAYS AHEAD OF SCHEDULE	DAYS BEHIND SCHEDULE

SAFETY AND INCIDENTS

SAFETY ISSUES THAT NEED TO BE ADDRESSED	ACCIDENTS / INCIDENTS / STEPS NEEDED TO RESOLVE

SUMMARY OF THE WORK DONE TODAY

IMPORTANT NOTES

NAME	SIGNATURE

TODAY LABOR

INITIALS	TRADE	START	FINISH	PAID HOURS	OVERTIME	COMPANY
☐ EMPLOYEE ☐ CONTRUCTOR		AM	PM			
☐ EMPLOYEE ☐ CONTRUCTOR		AM	PM			
☐ EMPLOYEE ☐ CONTRUCTOR		AM	PM			
☐ EMPLOYEE ☐ CONTRUCTOR		AM	PM			
☐ EMPLOYEE ☐ CONTRUCTOR		AM	PM			
☐ EMPLOYEE ☐ CONTRUCTOR		AM	PM			
☐ EMPLOYEE ☐ CONTRUCTOR		AM	PM			
☐ EMPLOYEE ☐ CONTRUCTOR		AM	PM			

EQUIPMENT ON SITE	NO. OF UNITE	WORKING YES / NO

HIRED EQUIPMENT	NO. OF UNITE	EQUIPMENT RENTED	FROM	RATE

NAME: ________________________   SIGNATURE: ________________________

MO TU WE TH FR SA SU

DATE: / /

PROJECT:

FOREMAN:

WEATHER

F°____ C°____ ____ AM ____ PM

HOURS DUE TO BAD WEATHER

ISSUED AND DELAYS

NOTE: _______________________________

COMPLETION DATE	DAYS AHEAD OF SCHEDULE	DAYS BEHIND SCHEDULE

SAFETY AND INCIDENTS

SAFETY ISSUES THAT NEED TO BE ADDRESSED	ACCIDENTS / INCIDENTS / STEPS NEEDED TO RESOLVE

SUMMARY OF THE WORK DONE TODAY

IMPORTANT NOTES

NAME	SIGNATURE

TODAY LABOR

INITIALS	TRADE	START	FINISH	PAID HOURS	OVERTIME	COMPANY
☐ EMPLOYEE ☐ CONTRUCTOR		AM	PM			
☐ EMPLOYEE ☐ CONTRUCTOR		AM	PM			
☐ EMPLOYEE ☐ CONTRUCTOR		AM	PM			
☐ EMPLOYEE ☐ CONTRUCTOR		AM	PM			
☐ EMPLOYEE ☐ CONTRUCTOR		AM	PM			
☐ EMPLOYEE ☐ CONTRUCTOR		AM	PM			
☐ EMPLOYEE ☐ CONTRUCTOR		AM	PM			
☐ EMPLOYEE ☐ CONTRUCTOR		AM	PM			

EQUIPMENT ON SITE	NO. OF UNITE	WORKING YES / NO

HIRED EQUIPMENT	NO. OF UNITE	EQUIPMENT RENTED	FROM	RATE

NAME: _______________________   SIGNATURE: _______________________

MO TU WE TH FR SA SU
☐   ☐   ☐   ☐   ☐   ☐   ☐

DATE: /   /

PROJECT:

FOREMAN:

WEATHER

F°_____ C°_____   _____ AM   _____ PM

HOURS DUE TO BAD WEATHER

ISSUED AND DELAYS

NOTE:

COMPLETION DATE	DAYS AHEAD OF SCHEDULE	DAYS BEHIND SCHEDULE

SAFETY AND INCIDENTS

SAFETY ISSUES THAT NEED TO BE ADDRESSED	ACCIDENTS / INCIDENTS / STEPS NEEDED TO RESOLVE

SUMMARY OF THE WORK DONE TODAY

IMPORTANT NOTES

NAME	SIGNATURE

TODAY LABOR

INITIALS	TRADE	START	FINISH	PAID HOURS	OVERTIME	COMPANY
☐ EMPLOYEE ☐ CONTRUCTOR		AM	PM			
☐ EMPLOYEE ☐ CONTRUCTOR		AM	PM			
☐ EMPLOYEE ☐ CONTRUCTOR		AM	PM			
☐ EMPLOYEE ☐ CONTRUCTOR		AM	PM			
☐ EMPLOYEE ☐ CONTRUCTOR		AM	PM			
☐ EMPLOYEE ☐ CONTRUCTOR		AM	PM			
☐ EMPLOYEE ☐ CONTRUCTOR		AM	PM			
☐ EMPLOYEE ☐ CONTRUCTOR		AM	PM			

EQUIPMENT ON SITE	NO. OF UNITE	WORKING YES / NO

HIRED EQUIPMENT	NO. OF UNITE	EQUIPMENT RENTED	FROM	RATE

NAME: ________________________   SIGNATURE: ________________________

MO   TU   WE   TH   FR   SA   SU
☐   ☐   ☐   ☐   ☐   ☐   ☐

DATE: /   /

PROJECT:

FOREMAN:

WEATHER

F°______ C°______   ______ AM ______ PM

HOURS DUE TO
BAD WEATHER

ISSUED AND DELAYS

NOTE:

COMPLETION DATE	DAYS AHEAD OF SCHEDULE	DAYS BEHIND SCHEDULE

SAFETY AND INCIDENTS

SAFETY ISSUES THAT NEED TO BE ADDRESSED	ACCIDENTS / INCIDENTS / STEPS NEEDED TO RESOLVE

SUMMARY OF THE WORK DONE TODAY

IMPORTANT NOTES

NAME	SIGNATURE

TODAY LABOR						
INITIALS	TRADE	START	FINISH	PAID HOURS	OVERTIME	COMPANY
☐ EMPLOYEE ☐ CONTRUCTOR		AM	PM			
☐ EMPLOYEE ☐ CONTRUCTOR		AM	PM			
☐ EMPLOYEE ☐ CONTRUCTOR		AM	PM			
☐ EMPLOYEE ☐ CONTRUCTOR		AM	PM			
☐ EMPLOYEE ☐ CONTRUCTOR		AM	PM			
☐ EMPLOYEE ☐ CONTRUCTOR		AM	PM			
☐ EMPLOYEE ☐ CONTRUCTOR		AM	PM			
☐ EMPLOYEE ☐ CONTRUCTOR		AM	PM			

EQUIPMENT ON SITE	NO. OF UNITE	WORKING YES / NO

HIRED EQUIPMENT	NO. OF UNITE	EQUIPMENT RENTED	FROM	RATE

NAME: ___________________________ SIGNATURE: ___________________________

MO TU WE TH FR SA SU
☐   ☐   ☐   ☐   ☐   ☐   ☐

DATE: /   /

PROJECT:

FOREMAN:

WEATHER

F°____ C°____   ____AM   ____PM

HOURS DUE TO BAD WEATHER	ISSUED AND DELAYS

NOTE: _______________________________________

COMPLETION DATE	DAYS AHEAD OF SCHEDULE	DAYS BEHIND SCHEDULE

SAFETY AND INCIDENTS

SAFETY ISSUES THAT NEED TO BE ADDRESSED	ACCIDENTS / INCIDENTS / STEPS NEEDED TO RESOLVE

SUMMARY OF THE WORK DONE TODAY

IMPORTANT NOTES

NAME	SIGNATURE

MO TU WE TH FR SA SU
☐   ☐   ☐   ☐   ☐   ☐   ☐

DATE: /   /

PROJECT:

FOREMAN:

WEATHER

F°____ C°____   ____ AM ____ PM

HOURS DUE TO BAD WEATHER	ISSUED AND DELAYS

NOTE: ____

COMPLETION DATE	DAYS AHEAD OF SCHEDULE	DAYS BEHIND SCHEDULE

SAFETY AND INCIDENTS

SAFETY ISSUES THAT NEED TO BE ADDRESSED	ACCIDENTS / INCIDENTS / STEPS NEEDED TO RESOLVE

SUMMARY OF THE WORK DONE TODAY

IMPORTANT NOTES

NAME	SIGNATURE

TODAY LABOR

INITIALS	TRADE	START	FINISH	PAID HOURS	OVERTIME	COMPANY
☐ EMPLOYEE ☐ CONTRUCTOR		AM	PM			
☐ EMPLOYEE ☐ CONTRUCTOR		AM	PM			
☐ EMPLOYEE ☐ CONTRUCTOR		AM	PM			
☐ EMPLOYEE ☐ CONTRUCTOR		AM	PM			
☐ EMPLOYEE ☐ CONTRUCTOR		AM	PM			
☐ EMPLOYEE ☐ CONTRUCTOR		AM	PM			
☐ EMPLOYEE ☐ CONTRUCTOR		AM	PM			
☐ EMPLOYEE ☐ CONTRUCTOR		AM	PM			

EQUIPMENT ON SITE	NO. OF UNITE	WORKING YES / NO

HIRED EQUIPMENT	NO. OF UNITE	EQUIPMENT RENTED	FROM	RATE

NAME: _______________________   SIGNATURE: _______________________

MO   TU   WE   TH   FR   SA   SU
☐   ☐   ☐   ☐   ☐   ☐   ☐

DATE: /   /

PROJECT:

FOREMAN:

WEATHER   F°_____ C°_____   _____ AM   _____ PM

HOURS DUE TO BAD WEATHER

ISSUED AND DELAYS

NOTE: ____

COMPLETION DATE	DAYS AHEAD OF SCHEDULE	DAYS BEHIND SCHEDULE

SAFETY AND INCIDENTS

SAFETY ISSUES THAT NEED TO BE ADDRESSED	ACCIDENTS / INCIDENTS / STEPS NEEDED TO RESOLVE

SUMMARY OF THE WORK DONE TODAY

IMPORTANT NOTES

NAME	SIGNATURE

TODAY LABOR

INITIALS	TRADE	START	FINISH	PAID HOURS	OVERTIME	COMPANY
☐ EMPLOYEE ☐ CONTRUCTOR		AM	PM			
☐ EMPLOYEE ☐ CONTRUCTOR		AM	PM			
☐ EMPLOYEE ☐ CONTRUCTOR		AM	PM			
☐ EMPLOYEE ☐ CONTRUCTOR		AM	PM			
☐ EMPLOYEE ☐ CONTRUCTOR		AM	PM			
☐ EMPLOYEE ☐ CONTRUCTOR		AM	PM			
☐ EMPLOYEE ☐ CONTRUCTOR		AM	PM			
☐ EMPLOYEE ☐ CONTRUCTOR		AM	PM			

EQUIPMENT ON SITE	NO. OF UNITE	WORKING YES / NO

HIRED EQUIPMENT	NO. OF UNITE	EQUIPMENT RENTED	FROM	RATE

NAME: _______________________   SIGNATURE: _______________________

MO   TU   WE   TH   FR   SA   SU
☐   ☐   ☐   ☐   ☐   ☐   ☐

DATE: /   /

PROJECT:

FOREMAN:

WEATHER

F°_____ C°_____   _____ AM   _____ PM

| HOURS DUE TO BAD WEATHER | ISSUED AND DELAYS |

NOTE: _______________________________________

COMPLETION DATE	DAYS AHEAD OF SCHEDULE	DAYS BEHIND SCHEDULE

SAFETY AND INCIDENTS

SAFETY ISSUES THAT NEED TO BE ADDRESSED	ACCIDENTS / INCIDENTS / STEPS NEEDED TO RESOLVE

SUMMARY OF THE WORK DONE TODAY

IMPORTANT NOTES

NAME	SIGNATURE

TODAY LABOR

INITIALS	TRADE	START	FINISH	PAID HOURS	OVERTIME	COMPANY
☐ EMPLOYEE ☐ CONTRUCTOR		AM	PM			
☐ EMPLOYEE ☐ CONTRUCTOR		AM	PM			
☐ EMPLOYEE ☐ CONTRUCTOR		AM	PM			
☐ EMPLOYEE ☐ CONTRUCTOR		AM	PM			
☐ EMPLOYEE ☐ CONTRUCTOR		AM	PM			
☐ EMPLOYEE ☐ CONTRUCTOR		AM	PM			
☐ EMPLOYEE ☐ CONTRUCTOR		AM	PM			
☐ EMPLOYEE ☐ CONTRUCTOR		AM	PM			

EQUIPMENT ON SITE	NO. OF UNITE	WORKING YES / NO

HIRED EQUIPMENT	NO. OF UNITE	EQUIPMENT RENTED	FROM	RATE

NAME: _______________________   SIGNATURE: _______________________

MO ☐ TU ☐ WE ☐ TH ☐ FR ☐ SA ☐ SU ☐

DATE: ___ / ___ / ___

PROJECT:

FOREMAN:

WEATHER

F° ___ C° ___ ___ AM ___ PM

HOURS DUE TO BAD WEATHER

ISSUED AND DELAYS

NOTE: _______________

COMPLETION DATE	DAYS AHEAD OF SCHEDULE	DAYS BEHIND SCHEDULE

SAFETY AND INCIDENTS

SAFETY ISSUES THAT NEED TO BE ADDRESSED	ACCIDENTS / INCIDENTS / STEPS NEEDED TO RESOLVE

SUMMARY OF THE WORK DONE TODAY

IMPORTANT NOTES

NAME	SIGNATURE

TODAY LABOR

INITIALS	TRADE	START	FINISH	PAID HOURS	OVERTIME	COMPANY
☐ EMPLOYEE ☐ CONTRUCTOR		AM	PM			
☐ EMPLOYEE ☐ CONTRUCTOR		AM	PM			
☐ EMPLOYEE ☐ CONTRUCTOR		AM	PM			
☐ EMPLOYEE ☐ CONTRUCTOR		AM	PM			
☐ EMPLOYEE ☐ CONTRUCTOR		AM	PM			
☐ EMPLOYEE ☐ CONTRUCTOR		AM	PM			
☐ EMPLOYEE ☐ CONTRUCTOR		AM	PM			
☐ EMPLOYEE ☐ CONTRUCTOR		AM	PM			

EQUIPMENT ON SITE	NO. OF UNITE	WORKING YES / NO

HIRED EQUIPMENT	NO. OF UNITE	EQUIPMENT RENTED	FROM	RATE

NAME: ______________________   SIGNATURE: ______________________

MO   TU   WE   TH   FR   SA   SU
☐   ☐   ☐   ☐   ☐   ☐   ☐

DATE: ___ / ___ / ___

PROJECT:

FOREMAN:

WEATHER   F°_____ C°_____   _____ AM   _____ PM

HOURS DUE TO BAD WEATHER

ISSUED AND DELAYS

NOTE: ____

COMPLETION DATE	DAYS AHEAD OF SCHEDULE	DAYS BEHIND SCHEDULE

SAFETY AND INCIDENTS

SAFETY ISSUES THAT NEED TO BE ADDRESSED	ACCIDENTS / INCIDENTS / STEPS NEEDED TO RESOLVE

SUMMARY OF THE WORK DONE TODAY

IMPORTANT NOTES

NAME	SIGNATURE

TODAY LABOR

INITIALS	TRADE	START	FINISH	PAID HOURS	OVERTIME	COMPANY
☐ EMPLOYEE ☐ CONTRUCTOR		AM	PM			
☐ EMPLOYEE ☐ CONTRUCTOR		AM	PM			
☐ EMPLOYEE ☐ CONTRUCTOR		AM	PM			
☐ EMPLOYEE ☐ CONTRUCTOR		AM	PM			
☐ EMPLOYEE ☐ CONTRUCTOR		AM	PM			
☐ EMPLOYEE ☐ CONTRUCTOR		AM	PM			
☐ EMPLOYEE ☐ CONTRUCTOR		AM	PM			
☐ EMPLOYEE ☐ CONTRUCTOR		AM	PM			

EQUIPMENT ON SITE	NO. OF UNITE	WORKING YES / NO

HIRED EQUIPMENT	NO. OF UNITE	EQUIPMENT RENTED	FROM	RATE

NAME: ________________________   SIGNATURE: ________________________

MO ☐ TU ☐ WE ☐ TH ☐ FR ☐ SA ☐ SU ☐

DATE: ___ / ___ / ___

PROJECT:

FOREMAN:

WEATHER

F° _______ C° _______ _______ AM _______ PM

| HOURS DUE TO BAD WEATHER | ISSUED AND DELAYS |

NOTE: ____

COMPLETION DATE	DAYS AHEAD OF SCHEDULE	DAYS BEHIND SCHEDULE

SAFETY AND INCIDENTS

SAFETY ISSUES THAT NEED TO BE ADDRESSED	ACCIDENTS / INCIDENTS / STEPS NEEDED TO RESOLVE

SUMMARY OF THE WORK DONE TODAY

____
____
____
____
____

IMPORTANT NOTES

____
____
____
____
____

NAME	SIGNATURE

TODAY LABOR

INITIALS	TRADE	START	FINISH	PAID HOURS	OVERTIME	COMPANY
☐ EMPLOYEE ☐ CONTRUCTOR		AM	PM			
☐ EMPLOYEE ☐ CONTRUCTOR		AM	PM			
☐ EMPLOYEE ☐ CONTRUCTOR		AM	PM			
☐ EMPLOYEE ☐ CONTRUCTOR		AM	PM			
☐ EMPLOYEE ☐ CONTRUCTOR		AM	PM			
☐ EMPLOYEE ☐ CONTRUCTOR		AM	PM			
☐ EMPLOYEE ☐ CONTRUCTOR		AM	PM			
☐ EMPLOYEE ☐ CONTRUCTOR		AM	PM			

EQUIPMENT ON SITE	NO. OF UNITE	WORKING YES / NO

HIRED EQUIPMENT	NO. OF UNITE	EQUIPMENT RENTED	FROM	RATE

NAME: ______________________________   SIGNATURE: ______________________________

MO   TU   WE   TH   FR   SA   SU
☐   ☐   ☐   ☐   ☐   ☐   ☐

DATE: ___ / ___ / ___

PROJECT:

FOREMAN:

WEATHER   F°___ C°___   ___ AM   ___ PM

HOURS DUE TO BAD WEATHER	ISSUED AND DELAYS

NOTE: ____

COMPLETION DATE	DAYS AHEAD OF SCHEDULE	DAYS BEHIND SCHEDULE

SAFETY AND INCIDENTS

SAFETY ISSUES THAT NEED TO BE ADDRESSED	ACCIDENTS / INCIDENTS / STEPS NEEDED TO RESOLVE

SUMMARY OF THE WORK DONE TODAY

IMPORTANT NOTES

NAME	SIGNATURE

TODAY LABOR

INITIALS	TRADE	START	FINISH	PAID HOURS	OVERTIME	COMPANY
☐ EMPLOYEE ☐ CONTRUCTOR		AM	PM			
☐ EMPLOYEE ☐ CONTRUCTOR		AM	PM			
☐ EMPLOYEE ☐ CONTRUCTOR		AM	PM			
☐ EMPLOYEE ☐ CONTRUCTOR		AM	PM			
☐ EMPLOYEE ☐ CONTRUCTOR		AM	PM			
☐ EMPLOYEE ☐ CONTRUCTOR		AM	PM			
☐ EMPLOYEE ☐ CONTRUCTOR		AM	PM			
☐ EMPLOYEE ☐ CONTRUCTOR		AM	PM			

EQUIPMENT ON SITE	NO. OF UNITE	WORKING YES / NO

HIRED EQUIPMENT	NO. OF UNITE	EQUIPMENT RENTED	FROM	RATE

NAME: ______________________   SIGNATURE: ______________________

MO TU WE TH FR SA SU
☐   ☐   ☐   ☐   ☐   ☐   ☐

DATE: /   /

PROJECT:

FOREMAN:

WEATHER

F°_____ C°_____   _____ AM _____ PM

HOURS DUE TO
BAD WEATHER

ISSUED AND DELAYS

NOTE: ____

COMPLETION DATE	DAYS AHEAD OF SCHEDULE	DAYS BEHIND SCHEDULE

SAFETY AND INCIDENTS

SAFETY ISSUES THAT NEED TO BE ADDRESSED	ACCIDENTS / INCIDENTS / STEPS NEEDED TO RESOLVE

SUMMARY OF THE WORK DONE TODAY

IMPORTANT NOTES

NAME	SIGNATURE

TODAY LABOR

INITIALS	TRADE	START	FINISH	PAID HOURS	OVERTIME	COMPANY
☐ EMPLOYEE ☐ CONTRUCTOR		AM	PM			
☐ EMPLOYEE ☐ CONTRUCTOR		AM	PM			
☐ EMPLOYEE ☐ CONTRUCTOR		AM	PM			
☐ EMPLOYEE ☐ CONTRUCTOR		AM	PM			
☐ EMPLOYEE ☐ CONTRUCTOR		AM	PM			
☐ EMPLOYEE ☐ CONTRUCTOR		AM	PM			
☐ EMPLOYEE ☐ CONTRUCTOR		AM	PM			
☐ EMPLOYEE ☐ CONTRUCTOR		AM	PM			

EQUIPMENT ON SITE	NO. OF UNITE	WORKING YES / NO

HIRED EQUIPMENT	NO. OF UNITE	EQUIPMENT RENTED	FROM	RATE

NAME: _______________________   SIGNATURE: _______________________

MO	TU	WE	TH	FR	SA	SU
☐	☐	☐	☐	☐	☐	☐

DATE: ____ / ____ / ____

PROJECT:

FOREMAN:

WEATHER

F° ______ C° ______   ______ AM ______ PM

HOURS DUE TO BAD WEATHER	ISSUED AND DELAYS

NOTE: ________________________________

COMPLETION DATE	DAYS AHEAD OF SCHEDULE	DAYS BEHIND SCHEDULE

SAFETY AND INCIDENTS

SAFETY ISSUES THAT NEED TO BE ADDRESSED	ACCIDENTS / INCIDENTS / STEPS NEEDED TO RESOLVE

SUMMARY OF THE WORK DONE TODAY

IMPORTANT NOTES

NAME	SIGNATURE

TODAY LABOR

INITIALS	TRADE	START	FINISH	PAID HOURS	OVERTIME	COMPANY
☐ EMPLOYEE ☐ CONTRUCTOR		AM	PM			
☐ EMPLOYEE ☐ CONTRUCTOR		AM	PM			
☐ EMPLOYEE ☐ CONTRUCTOR		AM	PM			
☐ EMPLOYEE ☐ CONTRUCTOR		AM	PM			
☐ EMPLOYEE ☐ CONTRUCTOR		AM	PM			
☐ EMPLOYEE ☐ CONTRUCTOR		AM	PM			
☐ EMPLOYEE ☐ CONTRUCTOR		AM	PM			
☐ EMPLOYEE ☐ CONTRUCTOR		AM	PM			

EQUIPMENT ON SITE	NO. OF UNITE	WORKING YES / NO

HIRED EQUIPMENT	NO. OF UNITE	EQUIPMENT RENTED	FROM	RATE

NAME: _______________________   SIGNATURE: _______________________

MO TU WE TH FR SA SU
☐ ☐ ☐ ☐ ☐ ☐ ☐

DATE: / /

PROJECT:

FOREMAN:

WEATHER

F°_____ C°_____ _____ AM _____ PM

HOURS DUE TO BAD WEATHER

ISSUED AND DELAYS

NOTE: _______________________________________

COMPLETION DATE	DAYS AHEAD OF SCHEDULE	DAYS BEHIND SCHEDULE

SAFETY AND INCIDENTS

SAFETY ISSUES THAT NEED TO BE ADDRESSED	ACCIDENTS / INCIDENTS / STEPS NEEDED TO RESOLVE

SUMMARY OF THE WORK DONE TODAY

IMPORTANT NOTES

NAME	SIGNATURE

TODAY LABOR

INITIALS	TRADE	START	FINISH	PAID HOURS	OVERTIME	COMPANY
☐ EMPLOYEE ☐ CONTRUCTOR		AM	PM			
☐ EMPLOYEE ☐ CONTRUCTOR		AM	PM			
☐ EMPLOYEE ☐ CONTRUCTOR		AM	PM			
☐ EMPLOYEE ☐ CONTRUCTOR		AM	PM			
☐ EMPLOYEE ☐ CONTRUCTOR		AM	PM			
☐ EMPLOYEE ☐ CONTRUCTOR		AM	PM			
☐ EMPLOYEE ☐ CONTRUCTOR		AM	PM			
☐ EMPLOYEE ☐ CONTRUCTOR		AM	PM			

EQUIPMENT ON SITE	NO. OF UNITE	WORKING YES / NO

HIRED EQUIPMENT	NO. OF UNITE	EQUIPMENT RENTED	FROM	RATE

NAME: ________________   SIGNATURE: ________________

MO   TU   WE   TH   FR   SA   SU
☐   ☐   ☐   ☐   ☐   ☐   ☐

DATE: /   /

PROJECT:

FOREMAN:

WEATHER

F°_____   C°_____   _____ AM   _____ PM

HOURS DUE TO
BAD WEATHER

ISSUED AND DELAYS

NOTE: ____

COMPLETION DATE	DAYS AHEAD OF SCHEDULE	DAYS BEHIND SCHEDULE

SAFETY AND INCIDENTS

SAFETY ISSUES THAT NEED TO BE ADDRESSED	ACCIDENTS / INCIDENTS / STEPS NEEDED TO RESOLVE

SUMMARY OF THE WORK DONE TODAY

IMPORTANT NOTES

NAME	SIGNATURE

TODAY LABOR						
INITIALS	TRADE	START	FINISH	PAID HOURS	OVERTIME	COMPANY
☐ EMPLOYEE ☐ CONTRUCTOR		AM	PM			
☐ EMPLOYEE ☐ CONTRUCTOR		AM	PM			
☐ EMPLOYEE ☐ CONTRUCTOR		AM	PM			
☐ EMPLOYEE ☐ CONTRUCTOR		AM	PM			
☐ EMPLOYEE ☐ CONTRUCTOR		AM	PM			
☐ EMPLOYEE ☐ CONTRUCTOR		AM	PM			
☐ EMPLOYEE ☐ CONTRUCTOR		AM	PM			
☐ EMPLOYEE ☐ CONTRUCTOR		AM	PM			

EQUIPMENT ON SITE	NO. OF UNITE	WORKING YES / NO

HIRED EQUIPMENT	NO. OF UNITE	EQUIPMENT RENTED	FROM	RATE

NAME: _______________________________   SIGNATURE: _______________________________

MO	TU	WE	TH	FR	SA	SU		DATE: / /

PROJECT:

FOREMAN:

WEATHER   F° ___ C° ___   ___ AM   ___ PM

| HOURS DUE TO BAD WEATHER | ISSUED AND DELAYS |

NOTE: ____

COMPLETION DATE	DAYS AHEAD OF SCHEDULE	DAYS BEHIND SCHEDULE

SAFETY AND INCIDENTS

SAFETY ISSUES THAT NEED TO BE ADDRESSED	ACCIDENTS / INCIDENTS / STEPS NEEDED TO RESOLVE

SUMMARY OF THE WORK DONE TODAY

IMPORTANT NOTES

NAME	SIGNATURE

<table>
<tr><td colspan="7" align="center">TODAY LABOR</td></tr>
<tr><td>INITIALS</td><td>TRADE</td><td>START</td><td>FINISH</td><td>PAID HOURS</td><td>OVERTIME</td><td>COMPANY</td></tr>
<tr><td>☐ EMPLOYEE
☐ CONTRUCTOR</td><td></td><td>AM</td><td>PM</td><td></td><td></td><td></td></tr>
<tr><td>☐ EMPLOYEE
☐ CONTRUCTOR</td><td></td><td>AM</td><td>PM</td><td></td><td></td><td></td></tr>
<tr><td>☐ EMPLOYEE
☐ CONTRUCTOR</td><td></td><td>AM</td><td>PM</td><td></td><td></td><td></td></tr>
<tr><td>☐ EMPLOYEE
☐ CONTRUCTOR</td><td></td><td>AM</td><td>PM</td><td></td><td></td><td></td></tr>
<tr><td>☐ EMPLOYEE
☐ CONTRUCTOR</td><td></td><td>AM</td><td>PM</td><td></td><td></td><td></td></tr>
<tr><td>☐ EMPLOYEE
☐ CONTRUCTOR</td><td></td><td>AM</td><td>PM</td><td></td><td></td><td></td></tr>
<tr><td>☐ EMPLOYEE
☐ CONTRUCTOR</td><td></td><td>AM</td><td>PM</td><td></td><td></td><td></td></tr>
<tr><td>☐ EMPLOYEE
☐ CONTRUCTOR</td><td></td><td>AM</td><td>PM</td><td></td><td></td><td></td></tr>
</table>

EQUIPMENT ON SITE	NO. OF UNITE	WORKING YES / NO

HIRED EQUIPMENT	NO. OF UNITE	EQUIPMENT RENTED	FROM	RATE

NAME: ________________________   SIGNATURE: ________________________

MO TU WE TH FR SA SU
☐   ☐   ☐   ☐   ☐   ☐   ☐

DATE: /   /

PROJECT:

FOREMAN:

WEATHER

F°_______ C°_______   _______ AM   _______ PM

HOURS DUE TO BAD WEATHER	ISSUED AND DELAYS

NOTE: ____

COMPLETION DATE	DAYS AHEAD OF SCHEDULE	DAYS BEHIND SCHEDULE

SAFETY AND INCIDENTS

SAFETY ISSUES THAT NEED TO BE ADDRESSED	ACCIDENTS / INCIDENTS / STEPS NEEDED TO RESOLVE

SUMMARY OF THE WORK DONE TODAY

IMPORTANT NOTES

NAME	SIGNATURE

INITIALS	TRADE	START	FINISH	PAID HOURS	OVERTIME	COMPANY
☐ EMPLOYEE ☐ CONTRUCTOR		AM	PM			
☐ EMPLOYEE ☐ CONTRUCTOR		AM	PM			
☐ EMPLOYEE ☐ CONTRUCTOR		AM	PM			
☐ EMPLOYEE ☐ CONTRUCTOR		AM	PM			
☐ EMPLOYEE ☐ CONTRUCTOR		AM	PM			
☐ EMPLOYEE ☐ CONTRUCTOR		AM	PM			
☐ EMPLOYEE ☐ CONTRUCTOR		AM	PM			
☐ EMPLOYEE ☐ CONTRUCTOR		AM	PM			

EQUIPMENT ON SITE	NO. OF UNITE	WORKING YES / NO

HIRED EQUIPMENT	NO. OF UNITE	EQUIPMENT RENTED	FROM	RATE

NAME: _______________________   SIGNATURE: _______________________

MO TU WE TH FR SA SU
☐   ☐   ☐   ☐   ☐   ☐   ☐

DATE: /   /

PROJECT:

FOREMAN:

WEATHER
F°_____ C°_____   _____AM   _____PM

HOURS DUE TO BAD WEATHER

ISSUED AND DELAYS

NOTE:

COMPLETION DATE	DAYS AHEAD OF SCHEDULE	DAYS BEHIND SCHEDULE

SAFETY AND INCIDENTS

SAFETY ISSUES THAT NEED TO BE ADDRESSED	ACCIDENTS / INCIDENTS / STEPS NEEDED TO RESOLVE

SUMMARY OF THE WORK DONE TODAY

IMPORTANT NOTES

NAME	SIGNATURE

TODAY LABOR

INITIALS	TRADE	START	FINISH	PAID HOURS	OVERTIME	COMPANY
☐ EMPLOYEE ☐ CONTRUCTOR		AM	PM			
☐ EMPLOYEE ☐ CONTRUCTOR		AM	PM			
☐ EMPLOYEE ☐ CONTRUCTOR		AM	PM			
☐ EMPLOYEE ☐ CONTRUCTOR		AM	PM			
☐ EMPLOYEE ☐ CONTRUCTOR		AM	PM			
☐ EMPLOYEE ☐ CONTRUCTOR		AM	PM			
☐ EMPLOYEE ☐ CONTRUCTOR		AM	PM			
☐ EMPLOYEE ☐ CONTRUCTOR		AM	PM			

EQUIPMENT ON SITE	NO. OF UNITE	WORKING YES / NO

HIRED EQUIPMENT	NO. OF UNITE	EQUIPMENT RENTED	FROM	RATE

NAME: ______________________   SIGNATURE: ______________________

MO TU WE TH FR SA SU
☐   ☐   ☐   ☐   ☐   ☐   ☐

DATE: ___ / ___ / ___

PROJECT:

FOREMAN:

WEATHER

F° ______ C° ______   ______ AM ______ PM

HOURS DUE TO BAD WEATHER

ISSUED AND DELAYS

NOTE: ____

COMPLETION DATE	DAYS AHEAD OF SCHEDULE	DAYS BEHIND SCHEDULE

SAFETY AND INCIDENTS

SAFETY ISSUES THAT NEED TO BE ADDRESSED	ACCIDENTS / INCIDENTS / STEPS NEEDED TO RESOLVE

SUMMARY OF THE WORK DONE TODAY

IMPORTANT NOTES

NAME	SIGNATURE

<table>
<tr><td colspan="7" align="center">TODAY LABOR</td></tr>
<tr><td>INITIALS</td><td>TRADE</td><td>START</td><td>FINISH</td><td>PAID HOURS</td><td>OVERTIME</td><td>COMPANY</td></tr>
<tr><td>☐ EMPLOYEE
☐ CONTRUCTOR</td><td></td><td>AM</td><td>PM</td><td></td><td></td><td></td></tr>
<tr><td>☐ EMPLOYEE
☐ CONTRUCTOR</td><td></td><td>AM</td><td>PM</td><td></td><td></td><td></td></tr>
<tr><td>☐ EMPLOYEE
☐ CONTRUCTOR</td><td></td><td>AM</td><td>PM</td><td></td><td></td><td></td></tr>
<tr><td>☐ EMPLOYEE
☐ CONTRUCTOR</td><td></td><td>AM</td><td>PM</td><td></td><td></td><td></td></tr>
<tr><td>☐ EMPLOYEE
☐ CONTRUCTOR</td><td></td><td>AM</td><td>PM</td><td></td><td></td><td></td></tr>
<tr><td>☐ EMPLOYEE
☐ CONTRUCTOR</td><td></td><td>AM</td><td>PM</td><td></td><td></td><td></td></tr>
<tr><td>☐ EMPLOYEE
☐ CONTRUCTOR</td><td></td><td>AM</td><td>PM</td><td></td><td></td><td></td></tr>
<tr><td>☐ EMPLOYEE
☐ CONTRUCTOR</td><td></td><td>AM</td><td>PM</td><td></td><td></td><td></td></tr>
</table>

EQUIPMENT ON SITE	NO. OF UNITE	WORKING YES / NO

HIRED EQUIPMENT	NO. OF UNITE	EQUIPMENT RENTED	FROM	RATE

NAME: _______________________ SIGNATURE: _______________________

MO TU WE TH FR SA SU
☐   ☐   ☐   ☐   ☐   ☐   ☐

DATE: /   /

PROJECT:

FOREMAN:

WEATHER

F°___ C°___   ___AM   ___PM

HOURS DUE TO BAD WEATHER	ISSUED AND DELAYS

NOTE: ____

COMPLETION DATE	DAYS AHEAD OF SCHEDULE	DAYS BEHIND SCHEDULE

SAFETY AND INCIDENTS

SAFETY ISSUES THAT NEED TO BE ADDRESSED	ACCIDENTS / INCIDENTS / STEPS NEEDED TO RESOLVE

SUMMARY OF THE WORK DONE TODAY

____
____
____
____
____

IMPORTANT NOTES

____
____
____
____
____

NAME	SIGNATURE

TODAY LABOR

INITIALS	TRADE	START	FINISH	PAID HOURS	OVERTIME	COMPANY
☐ EMPLOYEE ☐ CONTRUCTOR		AM	PM			
☐ EMPLOYEE ☐ CONTRUCTOR		AM	PM			
☐ EMPLOYEE ☐ CONTRUCTOR		AM	PM			
☐ EMPLOYEE ☐ CONTRUCTOR		AM	PM			
☐ EMPLOYEE ☐ CONTRUCTOR		AM	PM			
☐ EMPLOYEE ☐ CONTRUCTOR		AM	PM			
☐ EMPLOYEE ☐ CONTRUCTOR		AM	PM			
☐ EMPLOYEE ☐ CONTRUCTOR		AM	PM			

EQUIPMENT ON SITE	NO. OF UNITE	WORKING YES / NO

HIRED EQUIPMENT	NO. OF UNITE	EQUIPMENT RENTED	FROM	RATE

NAME: _______________________   SIGNATURE: _______________________

MO TU WE TH FR SA SU
☐   ☐   ☐   ☐   ☐   ☐   ☐

DATE: /   /

PROJECT:

FOREMAN:

WEATHER

F°______ C°______   ______ AM   ______ PM

HOURS DUE TO BAD WEATHER

ISSUED AND DELAYS

NOTE: ________________________________

COMPLETION DATE	DAYS AHEAD OF SCHEDULE	DAYS BEHIND SCHEDULE

SAFETY AND INCIDENTS

SAFETY ISSUES THAT NEED TO BE ADDRESSED	ACCIDENTS / INCIDENTS / STEPS NEEDED TO RESOLVE

SUMMARY OF THE WORK DONE TODAY

IMPORTANT NOTES

NAME	SIGNATURE

TODAY LABOR

INITIALS	TRADE	START	FINISH	PAID HOURS	OVERTIME	COMPANY
☐ EMPLOYEE ☐ CONTRUCTOR		AM	PM			
☐ EMPLOYEE ☐ CONTRUCTOR		AM	PM			
☐ EMPLOYEE ☐ CONTRUCTOR		AM	PM			
☐ EMPLOYEE ☐ CONTRUCTOR		AM	PM			
☐ EMPLOYEE ☐ CONTRUCTOR		AM	PM			
☐ EMPLOYEE ☐ CONTRUCTOR		AM	PM			
☐ EMPLOYEE ☐ CONTRUCTOR		AM	PM			
☐ EMPLOYEE ☐ CONTRUCTOR		AM	PM			

EQUIPMENT ON SITE	NO. OF UNITE	WORKING YES / NO

HIRED EQUIPMENT	NO. OF UNITE	EQUIPMENT RENTED	FROM	RATE

NAME: _______________________   SIGNATURE: _______________________

MO   TU   WE   TH   FR   SA   SU
☐   ☐   ☐   ☐   ☐   ☐   ☐

DATE: /   /

PROJECT:

FOREMAN:

WEATHER

F°____   C°____   ____ AM   ____ PM

HOURS DUE TO BAD WEATHER	ISSUED AND DELAYS

NOTE: ____

COMPLETION DATE	DAYS AHEAD OF SCHEDULE	DAYS BEHIND SCHEDULE

SAFETY AND INCIDENTS

SAFETY ISSUES THAT NEED TO BE ADDRESSED	ACCIDENTS / INCIDENTS / STEPS NEEDED TO RESOLVE

SUMMARY OF THE WORK DONE TODAY

IMPORTANT NOTES

NAME	SIGNATURE

<table>
<tr><td colspan="7" align="center">TODAY LABOR</td></tr>
<tr><td>INITIALS</td><td>TRADE</td><td>START</td><td>FINISH</td><td>PAID HOURS</td><td>OVERTIME</td><td>COMPANY</td></tr>
<tr><td>☐ EMPLOYEE
☐ CONTRUCTOR</td><td></td><td>AM</td><td>PM</td><td></td><td></td><td></td></tr>
<tr><td>☐ EMPLOYEE
☐ CONTRUCTOR</td><td></td><td>AM</td><td>PM</td><td></td><td></td><td></td></tr>
<tr><td>☐ EMPLOYEE
☐ CONTRUCTOR</td><td></td><td>AM</td><td>PM</td><td></td><td></td><td></td></tr>
<tr><td>☐ EMPLOYEE
☐ CONTRUCTOR</td><td></td><td>AM</td><td>PM</td><td></td><td></td><td></td></tr>
<tr><td>☐ EMPLOYEE
☐ CONTRUCTOR</td><td></td><td>AM</td><td>PM</td><td></td><td></td><td></td></tr>
<tr><td>☐ EMPLOYEE
☐ CONTRUCTOR</td><td></td><td>AM</td><td>PM</td><td></td><td></td><td></td></tr>
<tr><td>☐ EMPLOYEE
☐ CONTRUCTOR</td><td></td><td>AM</td><td>PM</td><td></td><td></td><td></td></tr>
<tr><td>☐ EMPLOYEE
☐ CONTRUCTOR</td><td></td><td>AM</td><td>PM</td><td></td><td></td><td></td></tr>
</table>

EQUIPMENT ON SITE	NO. OF UNITE	WORKING YES / NO

HIRED EQUIPMENT	NO. OF UNITE	EQUIPMENT RENTED	FROM	RATE

NAME: _______________________   SIGNATURE: _______________________

MO   TU   WE   TH   FR   SA   SU
☐   ☐   ☐   ☐   ☐   ☐   ☐

DATE: ___ / ___ / ___

PROJECT:

FOREMAN:

WEATHER   F° ____   C° ____   ____ AM   ____ PM

HOURS DUE TO BAD WEATHER	ISSUED AND DELAYS

NOTE: ____

COMPLETION DATE	DAYS AHEAD OF SCHEDULE	DAYS BEHIND SCHEDULE

SAFETY AND INCIDENTS

SAFETY ISSUES THAT NEED TO BE ADDRESSED	ACCIDENTS / INCIDENTS / STEPS NEEDED TO RESOLVE

SUMMARY OF THE WORK DONE TODAY

IMPORTANT NOTES

NAME	SIGNATURE

TODAY LABOR

INITIALS	TRADE	START	FINISH	PAID HOURS	OVERTIME	COMPANY
☐ EMPLOYEE ☐ CONTRUCTOR		AM	PM			
☐ EMPLOYEE ☐ CONTRUCTOR		AM	PM			
☐ EMPLOYEE ☐ CONTRUCTOR		AM	PM			
☐ EMPLOYEE ☐ CONTRUCTOR		AM	PM			
☐ EMPLOYEE ☐ CONTRUCTOR		AM	PM			
☐ EMPLOYEE ☐ CONTRUCTOR		AM	PM			
☐ EMPLOYEE ☐ CONTRUCTOR		AM	PM			
☐ EMPLOYEE ☐ CONTRUCTOR		AM	PM			

EQUIPMENT ON SITE	NO. OF UNITE	WORKING YES / NO

HIRED EQUIPMENT	NO. OF UNITE	EQUIPMENT RENTED	FROM	RATE

NAME: _______________________   SIGNATURE: _______________________

MO   TU   WE   TH   FR   SA   SU
☐   ☐   ☐   ☐   ☐   ☐   ☐

DATE: /   /

PROJECT:

FOREMAN:

WEATHER

F°_____ C°_____   _____ AM   _____ PM

HOURS DUE TO BAD WEATHER	ISSUED AND DELAYS

NOTE: _______________

COMPLETION DATE	DAYS AHEAD OF SCHEDULE	DAYS BEHIND SCHEDULE

SAFETY AND INCIDENTS

SAFETY ISSUES THAT NEED TO BE ADDRESSED	ACCIDENTS / INCIDENTS / STEPS NEEDED TO RESOLVE

SUMMARY OF THE WORK DONE TODAY

IMPORTANT NOTES

NAME	SIGNATURE

TODAY LABOR

INITIALS	TRADE	START	FINISH	PAID HOURS	OVERTIME	COMPANY
☐ EMPLOYEE ☐ CONTRUCTOR		AM	PM			
☐ EMPLOYEE ☐ CONTRUCTOR		AM	PM			
☐ EMPLOYEE ☐ CONTRUCTOR		AM	PM			
☐ EMPLOYEE ☐ CONTRUCTOR		AM	PM			
☐ EMPLOYEE ☐ CONTRUCTOR		AM	PM			
☐ EMPLOYEE ☐ CONTRUCTOR		AM	PM			
☐ EMPLOYEE ☐ CONTRUCTOR		AM	PM			
☐ EMPLOYEE ☐ CONTRUCTOR		AM	PM			

EQUIPMENT ON SITE	NO. OF UNITE	WORKING YES / NO

HIRED EQUIPMENT	NO. OF UNITE	EQUIPMENT RENTED	FROM	RATE

NAME: ___________________   SIGNATURE: ___________________

MO   TU   WE   TH   FR   SA   SU
☐   ☐   ☐   ☐   ☐   ☐   ☐

DATE: /   /

PROJECT:

FOREMAN:

WEATHER

F°____   C°____   ____ AM   ____ PM

HOURS DUE TO BAD WEATHER	ISSUED AND DELAYS

NOTE: ____

COMPLETION DATE	DAYS AHEAD OF SCHEDULE	DAYS BEHIND SCHEDULE

SAFETY AND INCIDENTS

SAFETY ISSUES THAT NEED TO BE ADDRESSED	ACCIDENTS / INCIDENTS / STEPS NEEDED TO RESOLVE

SUMMARY OF THE WORK DONE TODAY

IMPORTANT NOTES

NAME	SIGNATURE

<table>
<tr><th colspan="7" align="center">TODAY LABOR</th></tr>
<tr><th>INITIALS</th><th>TRADE</th><th>START</th><th>FINISH</th><th>PAID HOURS</th><th>OVERTIME</th><th>COMPANY</th></tr>
<tr><td>☐ EMPLOYEE
☐ CONTRUCTOR</td><td></td><td>AM</td><td>PM</td><td></td><td></td><td></td></tr>
<tr><td>☐ EMPLOYEE
☐ CONTRUCTOR</td><td></td><td>AM</td><td>PM</td><td></td><td></td><td></td></tr>
<tr><td>☐ EMPLOYEE
☐ CONTRUCTOR</td><td></td><td>AM</td><td>PM</td><td></td><td></td><td></td></tr>
<tr><td>☐ EMPLOYEE
☐ CONTRUCTOR</td><td></td><td>AM</td><td>PM</td><td></td><td></td><td></td></tr>
<tr><td>☐ EMPLOYEE
☐ CONTRUCTOR</td><td></td><td>AM</td><td>PM</td><td></td><td></td><td></td></tr>
<tr><td>☐ EMPLOYEE
☐ CONTRUCTOR</td><td></td><td>AM</td><td>PM</td><td></td><td></td><td></td></tr>
<tr><td>☐ EMPLOYEE
☐ CONTRUCTOR</td><td></td><td>AM</td><td>PM</td><td></td><td></td><td></td></tr>
<tr><td>☐ EMPLOYEE
☐ CONTRUCTOR</td><td></td><td>AM</td><td>PM</td><td></td><td></td><td></td></tr>
</table>

EQUIPMENT ON SITE	NO. OF UNITE	WORKING YES / NO

HIRED EQUIPMENT	NO. OF UNITE	EQUIPMENT RENTED	FROM	RATE

NAME: _______________________   SIGNATURE: _______________________

MO TU WE TH FR SA SU
☐   ☐   ☐   ☐   ☐   ☐   ☐

DATE: ___ / ___ / ___

PROJECT:

FOREMAN:

WEATHER   F°____ C°____ ____AM ____PM

| HOURS DUE TO BAD WEATHER | ISSUED AND DELAYS |

NOTE: ______________________________

COMPLETION DATE	DAYS AHEAD OF SCHEDULE	DAYS BEHIND SCHEDULE

SAFETY AND INCIDENTS

SAFETY ISSUES THAT NEED TO BE ADDRESSED	ACCIDENTS / INCIDENTS / STEPS NEEDED TO RESOLVE

SUMMARY OF THE WORK DONE TODAY

IMPORTANT NOTES

NAME	SIGNATURE

TODAY LABOR

INITIALS	TRADE	START	FINISH	PAID HOURS	OVERTIME	COMPANY
☐ EMPLOYEE ☐ CONTRUCTOR		AM	PM			
☐ EMPLOYEE ☐ CONTRUCTOR		AM	PM			
☐ EMPLOYEE ☐ CONTRUCTOR		AM	PM			
☐ EMPLOYEE ☐ CONTRUCTOR		AM	PM			
☐ EMPLOYEE ☐ CONTRUCTOR		AM	PM			
☐ EMPLOYEE ☐ CONTRUCTOR		AM	PM			
☐ EMPLOYEE ☐ CONTRUCTOR		AM	PM			
☐ EMPLOYEE ☐ CONTRUCTOR		AM	PM			

EQUIPMENT ON SITE	NO. OF UNITE	WORKING YES / NO

HIRED EQUIPMENT	NO. OF UNITE	EQUIPMENT RENTED	FROM	RATE

NAME: ________________________   SIGNATURE: ________________________

MO TU WE TH FR SA SU
☐   ☐   ☐   ☐   ☐   ☐   ☐

DATE: /   /

PROJECT:

FOREMAN:

WEATHER

F°______ C°______   ______ AM   ______ PM

NOTE: ____

HOURS DUE TO BAD WEATHER

ISSUED AND DELAYS

COMPLETION DATE	DAYS AHEAD OF SCHEDULE	DAYS BEHIND SCHEDULE

SAFETY AND INCIDENTS

SAFETY ISSUES THAT NEED TO BE ADDRESSED	ACCIDENTS / INCIDENTS / STEPS NEEDED TO RESOLVE

SUMMARY OF THE WORK DONE TODAY

IMPORTANT NOTES

NAME	SIGNATURE

TODAY LABOR

INITIALS	TRADE	START	FINISH	PAID HOURS	OVERTIME	COMPANY
☐ EMPLOYEE ☐ CONTRUCTOR		AM	PM			
☐ EMPLOYEE ☐ CONTRUCTOR		AM	PM			
☐ EMPLOYEE ☐ CONTRUCTOR		AM	PM			
☐ EMPLOYEE ☐ CONTRUCTOR		AM	PM			
☐ EMPLOYEE ☐ CONTRUCTOR		AM	PM			
☐ EMPLOYEE ☐ CONTRUCTOR		AM	PM			
☐ EMPLOYEE ☐ CONTRUCTOR		AM	PM			
☐ EMPLOYEE ☐ CONTRUCTOR		AM	PM			

EQUIPMENT ON SITE	NO. OF UNITE	WORKING YES / NO

HIRED EQUIPMENT	NO. OF UNITE	EQUIPMENT RENTED	FROM	RATE

NAME: _______________________   SIGNATURE: _______________________

MO   TU   WE   TH   FR   SA   SU
☐   ☐   ☐   ☐   ☐   ☐   ☐

DATE: /   /

PROJECT:

FOREMAN:

WEATHER

F°_____ C°_____   _____ AM   _____ PM

HOURS DUE TO
BAD WEATHER

ISSUED AND DELAYS

NOTE: _______________________________________

COMPLETION DATE	DAYS AHEAD OF SCHEDULE	DAYS BEHIND SCHEDULE

SAFETY AND INCIDENTS

SAFETY ISSUES THAT NEED TO BE ADDRESSED	ACCIDENTS / INCIDENTS / STEPS NEEDED TO RESOLVE

SUMMARY OF THE WORK DONE TODAY

IMPORTANT NOTES

NAME	SIGNATURE

TODAY LABOR

INITIALS	TRADE	START	FINISH	PAID HOURS	OVERTIME	COMPANY
☐ EMPLOYEE ☐ CONTRUCTOR		AM	PM			
☐ EMPLOYEE ☐ CONTRUCTOR		AM	PM			
☐ EMPLOYEE ☐ CONTRUCTOR		AM	PM			
☐ EMPLOYEE ☐ CONTRUCTOR		AM	PM			
☐ EMPLOYEE ☐ CONTRUCTOR		AM	PM			
☐ EMPLOYEE ☐ CONTRUCTOR		AM	PM			
☐ EMPLOYEE ☐ CONTRUCTOR		AM	PM			
☐ EMPLOYEE ☐ CONTRUCTOR		AM	PM			

EQUIPMENT ON SITE	NO. OF UNITE	WORKING YES / NO

HIRED EQUIPMENT	NO. OF UNITE	EQUIPMENT RENTED	FROM	RATE

NAME: _______________________   SIGNATURE: _______________________

MO ☐ TU ☐ WE ☐ TH ☐ FR ☐ SA ☐ SU ☐

DATE: ___ / ___ / ___

PROJECT:

FOREMAN:

WEATHER   F° ___   C° ___   ___ AM   ___ PM

HOURS DUE TO BAD WEATHER	ISSUED AND DELAYS

NOTE: _______________________________________

COMPLETION DATE	DAYS AHEAD OF SCHEDULE	DAYS BEHIND SCHEDULE

SAFETY AND INCIDENTS

SAFETY ISSUES THAT NEED TO BE ADDRESSED	ACCIDENTS / INCIDENTS / STEPS NEEDED TO RESOLVE

SUMMARY OF THE WORK DONE TODAY

IMPORTANT NOTES

NAME	SIGNATURE

TODAY LABOR

INITIALS	TRADE	START	FINISH	PAID HOURS	OVERTIME	COMPANY
☐ EMPLOYEE ☐ CONTRUCTOR		AM	PM			
☐ EMPLOYEE ☐ CONTRUCTOR		AM	PM			
☐ EMPLOYEE ☐ CONTRUCTOR		AM	PM			
☐ EMPLOYEE ☐ CONTRUCTOR		AM	PM			
☐ EMPLOYEE ☐ CONTRUCTOR		AM	PM			
☐ EMPLOYEE ☐ CONTRUCTOR		AM	PM			
☐ EMPLOYEE ☐ CONTRUCTOR		AM	PM			
☐ EMPLOYEE ☐ CONTRUCTOR		AM	PM			

EQUIPMENT ON SITE	NO. OF UNITE	WORKING YES / NO

HIRED EQUIPMENT	NO. OF UNITE	EQUIPMENT RENTED	FROM	RATE

NAME: _______________   SIGNATURE: _______________

MO   TU   WE   TH   FR   SA   SU
☐   ☐   ☐   ☐   ☐   ☐   ☐

DATE: /   /

PROJECT:

FOREMAN:

WEATHER

F°_____ C°_____   _____ AM   _____ PM

HOURS DUE TO BAD WEATHER	ISSUED AND DELAYS

NOTE: ____

COMPLETION DATE	DAYS AHEAD OF SCHEDULE	DAYS BEHIND SCHEDULE

SAFETY AND INCIDENTS

SAFETY ISSUES THAT NEED TO BE ADDRESSED	ACCIDENTS / INCIDENTS / STEPS NEEDED TO RESOLVE

SUMMARY OF THE WORK DONE TODAY

IMPORTANT NOTES

NAME	SIGNATURE

TODAY LABOR

INITIALS	TRADE	START	FINISH	PAID HOURS	OVERTIME	COMPANY
☐ EMPLOYEE ☐ CONTRUCTOR		AM	PM			
☐ EMPLOYEE ☐ CONTRUCTOR		AM	PM			
☐ EMPLOYEE ☐ CONTRUCTOR		AM	PM			
☐ EMPLOYEE ☐ CONTRUCTOR		AM	PM			
☐ EMPLOYEE ☐ CONTRUCTOR		AM	PM			
☐ EMPLOYEE ☐ CONTRUCTOR		AM	PM			
☐ EMPLOYEE ☐ CONTRUCTOR		AM	PM			
☐ EMPLOYEE ☐ CONTRUCTOR		AM	PM			

EQUIPMENT ON SITE	NO. OF UNITE	WORKING YES / NO

HIRED EQUIPMENT	NO. OF UNITE	EQUIPMENT RENTED	FROM	RATE

NAME: _______________________   SIGNATURE: _______________________

MO TU WE TH FR SA SU
☐   ☐   ☐   ☐   ☐   ☐   ☐

DATE: ___ / ___ / ___

PROJECT:

FOREMAN:

WEATHER F° ____ C° ____ ____ AM ____ PM

HOURS DUE TO BAD WEATHER	ISSUED AND DELAYS

NOTE: ____

COMPLETION DATE	DAYS AHEAD OF SCHEDULE	DAYS BEHIND SCHEDULE

SAFETY AND INCIDENTS

SAFETY ISSUES THAT NEED TO BE ADDRESSED	ACCIDENTS / INCIDENTS / STEPS NEEDED TO RESOLVE

SUMMARY OF THE WORK DONE TODAY

IMPORTANT NOTES

NAME	SIGNATURE

TODAY LABOR

INITIALS	TRADE	START	FINISH	PAID HOURS	OVERTIME	COMPANY
☐ EMPLOYEE ☐ CONTRUCTOR		AM	PM			
☐ EMPLOYEE ☐ CONTRUCTOR		AM	PM			
☐ EMPLOYEE ☐ CONTRUCTOR		AM	PM			
☐ EMPLOYEE ☐ CONTRUCTOR		AM	PM			
☐ EMPLOYEE ☐ CONTRUCTOR		AM	PM			
☐ EMPLOYEE ☐ CONTRUCTOR		AM	PM			
☐ EMPLOYEE ☐ CONTRUCTOR		AM	PM			
☐ EMPLOYEE ☐ CONTRUCTOR		AM	PM			

EQUIPMENT ON SITE	NO. OF UNITE	WORKING YES / NO

HIRED EQUIPMENT	NO. OF UNITE	EQUIPMENT RENTED	FROM	RATE

NAME: _______________________   SIGNATURE: _______________________

MO TU WE TH FR SA SU
☐   ☐   ☐   ☐   ☐   ☐   ☐

DATE: /   /

PROJECT:

FOREMAN:

WEATHER

F°____ C°____   ____ AM   ____ PM

HOURS DUE TO
BAD WEATHER

ISSUED AND DELAYS

NOTE:

COMPLETION DATE	DAYS AHEAD OF SCHEDULE	DAYS BEHIND SCHEDULE

SAFETY AND INCIDENTS

SAFETY ISSUES THAT NEED TO BE ADDRESSED	ACCIDENTS / INCIDENTS / STEPS NEEDED TO RESOLVE

SUMMARY OF THE WORK DONE TODAY

IMPORTANT NOTES

NAME	SIGNATURE

TODAY LABOR

INITIALS	TRADE	START	FINISH	PAID HOURS	OVERTIME	COMPANY
☐ EMPLOYEE ☐ CONTRUCTOR		AM	PM			
☐ EMPLOYEE ☐ CONTRUCTOR		AM	PM			
☐ EMPLOYEE ☐ CONTRUCTOR		AM	PM			
☐ EMPLOYEE ☐ CONTRUCTOR		AM	PM			
☐ EMPLOYEE ☐ CONTRUCTOR		AM	PM			
☐ EMPLOYEE ☐ CONTRUCTOR		AM	PM			
☐ EMPLOYEE ☐ CONTRUCTOR		AM	PM			
☐ EMPLOYEE ☐ CONTRUCTOR		AM	PM			

EQUIPMENT ON SITE	NO. OF UNITE	WORKING YES / NO

HIRED EQUIPMENT	NO. OF UNITE	EQUIPMENT RENTED	FROM	RATE

NAME: _______________________________   SIGNATURE: _______________________________

MO TU WE TH FR SA SU
☐   ☐   ☐   ☐   ☐   ☐   ☐

DATE: /   /

PROJECT:

FOREMAN:

WEATHER

F°_____ C°_____   _____ AM   _____ PM

HOURS DUE TO BAD WEATHER

ISSUED AND DELAYS

NOTE: ____

COMPLETION DATE	DAYS AHEAD OF SCHEDULE	DAYS BEHIND SCHEDULE

SAFETY AND INCIDENTS

SAFETY ISSUES THAT NEED TO BE ADDRESSED	ACCIDENTS / INCIDENTS / STEPS NEEDED TO RESOLVE

SUMMARY OF THE WORK DONE TODAY

IMPORTANT NOTES

NAME	SIGNATURE

TODAY LABOR

INITIALS	TRADE	START	FINISH	PAID HOURS	OVERTIME	COMPANY
☐ EMPLOYEE ☐ CONTRUCTOR		AM	PM			
☐ EMPLOYEE ☐ CONTRUCTOR		AM	PM			
☐ EMPLOYEE ☐ CONTRUCTOR		AM	PM			
☐ EMPLOYEE ☐ CONTRUCTOR		AM	PM			
☐ EMPLOYEE ☐ CONTRUCTOR		AM	PM			
☐ EMPLOYEE ☐ CONTRUCTOR		AM	PM			
☐ EMPLOYEE ☐ CONTRUCTOR		AM	PM			
☐ EMPLOYEE ☐ CONTRUCTOR		AM	PM			

EQUIPMENT ON SITE	NO. OF UNITE	WORKING YES / NO

HIRED EQUIPMENT	NO. OF UNITE	EQUIPMENT RENTED	FROM	RATE

NAME: ______________________   SIGNATURE: ______________________

MO TU WE TH FR SA SU
☐   ☐   ☐   ☐   ☐   ☐   ☐

DATE: /   /

PROJECT:

FOREMAN:

WEATHER   F°____ C°____   ____ AM   ____ PM

HOURS DUE TO BAD WEATHER	ISSUED AND DELAYS

NOTE: ____________________

COMPLETION DATE	DAYS AHEAD OF SCHEDULE	DAYS BEHIND SCHEDULE

SAFETY AND INCIDENTS

SAFETY ISSUES THAT NEED TO BE ADDRESSED	ACCIDENTS / INCIDENTS / STEPS NEEDED TO RESOLVE

SUMMARY OF THE WORK DONE TODAY

IMPORTANT NOTES

NAME	SIGNATURE

TODAY LABOR

INITIALS	TRADE	START	FINISH	PAID HOURS	OVERTIME	COMPANY
☐ EMPLOYEE ☐ CONTRUCTOR		AM	PM			
☐ EMPLOYEE ☐ CONTRUCTOR		AM	PM			
☐ EMPLOYEE ☐ CONTRUCTOR		AM	PM			
☐ EMPLOYEE ☐ CONTRUCTOR		AM	PM			
☐ EMPLOYEE ☐ CONTRUCTOR		AM	PM			
☐ EMPLOYEE ☐ CONTRUCTOR		AM	PM			
☐ EMPLOYEE ☐ CONTRUCTOR		AM	PM			
☐ EMPLOYEE ☐ CONTRUCTOR		AM	PM			

EQUIPMENT ON SITE	NO. OF UNITE	WORKING YES / NO

HIRED EQUIPMENT	NO. OF UNITE	EQUIPMENT RENTED	FROM	RATE

NAME: ______________________________   SIGNATURE: ______________________________

MO TU WE TH FR SA SU
☐   ☐   ☐   ☐   ☐   ☐   ☐

DATE: ___ / ___ / ___

PROJECT:

FOREMAN:

WEATHER

F° _____ C° _____   _____ AM _____ PM

HOURS DUE TO BAD WEATHER	ISSUED AND DELAYS

NOTE: ____

COMPLETION DATE	DAYS AHEAD OF SCHEDULE	DAYS BEHIND SCHEDULE

SAFETY AND INCIDENTS

SAFETY ISSUES THAT NEED TO BE ADDRESSED	ACCIDENTS / INCIDENTS / STEPS NEEDED TO RESOLVE

SUMMARY OF THE WORK DONE TODAY

IMPORTANT NOTES

NAME	SIGNATURE

TODAY LABOR

INITIALS	TRADE	START	FINISH	PAID HOURS	OVERTIME	COMPANY
☐ EMPLOYEE ☐ CONTRUCTOR		AM	PM			
☐ EMPLOYEE ☐ CONTRUCTOR		AM	PM			
☐ EMPLOYEE ☐ CONTRUCTOR		AM	PM			
☐ EMPLOYEE ☐ CONTRUCTOR		AM	PM			
☐ EMPLOYEE ☐ CONTRUCTOR		AM	PM			
☐ EMPLOYEE ☐ CONTRUCTOR		AM	PM			
☐ EMPLOYEE ☐ CONTRUCTOR		AM	PM			
☐ EMPLOYEE ☐ CONTRUCTOR		AM	PM			

EQUIPMENT ON SITE	NO. OF UNITE	WORKING YES / NO

HIRED EQUIPMENT	NO. OF UNITE	EQUIPMENT RENTED	FROM	RATE

NAME: __________________________   SIGNATURE: __________________________

MO ☐ TU ☐ WE ☐ TH ☐ FR ☐ SA ☐ SU ☐

DATE: ___ / ___ / ___

PROJECT:

FOREMAN:

WEATHER   F° ___   C° ___   ___ AM   ___ PM

HOURS DUE TO BAD WEATHER	ISSUED AND DELAYS

NOTE: ____

COMPLETION DATE	DAYS AHEAD OF SCHEDULE	DAYS BEHIND SCHEDULE

SAFETY AND INCIDENTS

SAFETY ISSUES THAT NEED TO BE ADDRESSED	ACCIDENTS / INCIDENTS / STEPS NEEDED TO RESOLVE

SUMMARY OF THE WORK DONE TODAY

IMPORTANT NOTES

NAME	SIGNATURE

TODAY LABOR

INITIALS	TRADE	START	FINISH	PAID HOURS	OVERTIME	COMPANY
☐ EMPLOYEE ☐ CONTRUCTOR		AM	PM			
☐ EMPLOYEE ☐ CONTRUCTOR		AM	PM			
☐ EMPLOYEE ☐ CONTRUCTOR		AM	PM			
☐ EMPLOYEE ☐ CONTRUCTOR		AM	PM			
☐ EMPLOYEE ☐ CONTRUCTOR		AM	PM			
☐ EMPLOYEE ☐ CONTRUCTOR		AM	PM			
☐ EMPLOYEE ☐ CONTRUCTOR		AM	PM			
☐ EMPLOYEE ☐ CONTRUCTOR		AM	PM			

EQUIPMENT ON SITE	NO. OF UNITE	WORKING YES / NO

HIRED EQUIPMENT	NO. OF UNITE	EQUIPMENT RENTED	FROM	RATE

NAME: _______________________   SIGNATURE: _______________________

MO   TU   WE   TH   FR   SA   SU
☐   ☐   ☐   ☐   ☐   ☐   ☐

DATE: ___ / ___ / ___

PROJECT:

FOREMAN:

WEATHER   F° _____   C° _____   _____ AM   _____ PM

HOURS DUE TO BAD WEATHER	ISSUED AND DELAYS

NOTE: ____

COMPLETION DATE	DAYS AHEAD OF SCHEDULE	DAYS BEHIND SCHEDULE

SAFETY AND INCIDENTS

SAFETY ISSUES THAT NEED TO BE ADDRESSED	ACCIDENTS / INCIDENTS / STEPS NEEDED TO RESOLVE

SUMMARY OF THE WORK DONE TODAY

IMPORTANT NOTES

NAME	SIGNATURE

TODAY LABOR

INITIALS	TRADE	START	FINISH	PAID HOURS	OVERTIME	COMPANY
☐ EMPLOYEE ☐ CONTRUCTOR		AM	PM			
☐ EMPLOYEE ☐ CONTRUCTOR		AM	PM			
☐ EMPLOYEE ☐ CONTRUCTOR		AM	PM			
☐ EMPLOYEE ☐ CONTRUCTOR		AM	PM			
☐ EMPLOYEE ☐ CONTRUCTOR		AM	PM			
☐ EMPLOYEE ☐ CONTRUCTOR		AM	PM			
☐ EMPLOYEE ☐ CONTRUCTOR		AM	PM			
☐ EMPLOYEE ☐ CONTRUCTOR		AM	PM			

EQUIPMENT ON SITE	NO. OF UNITE	WORKING YES / NO

HIRED EQUIPMENT	NO. OF UNITE	EQUIPMENT RENTED	FROM	RATE

NAME: _______________________   SIGNATURE: _______________________

MO TU WE TH FR SA SU
☐   ☐   ☐   ☐   ☐   ☐   ☐

DATE: /   /

PROJECT:

FOREMAN:

WEATHER

F°_____ C°_____   _____ AM _____ PM

HOURS DUE TO BAD WEATHER	ISSUED AND DELAYS

NOTE: ____________________________________

COMPLETION DATE	DAYS AHEAD OF SCHEDULE	DAYS BEHIND SCHEDULE

SAFETY AND INCIDENTS

SAFETY ISSUES THAT NEED TO BE ADDRESSED	ACCIDENTS / INCIDENTS / STEPS NEEDED TO RESOLVE

SUMMARY OF THE WORK DONE TODAY

IMPORTANT NOTES

NAME	SIGNATURE

TODAY LABOR

INITIALS	TRADE	START	FINISH	PAID HOURS	OVERTIME	COMPANY
☐ EMPLOYEE ☐ CONTRUCTOR		AM	PM			
☐ EMPLOYEE ☐ CONTRUCTOR		AM	PM			
☐ EMPLOYEE ☐ CONTRUCTOR		AM	PM			
☐ EMPLOYEE ☐ CONTRUCTOR		AM	PM			
☐ EMPLOYEE ☐ CONTRUCTOR		AM	PM			
☐ EMPLOYEE ☐ CONTRUCTOR		AM	PM			
☐ EMPLOYEE ☐ CONTRUCTOR		AM	PM			
☐ EMPLOYEE ☐ CONTRUCTOR		AM	PM			

EQUIPMENT ON SITE	NO. OF UNITE	WORKING YES / NO

HIRED EQUIPMENT	NO. OF UNITE	EQUIPMENT RENTED	FROM	RATE

NAME: _______________________   SIGNATURE: _______________________

MO TU WE TH FR SA SU
☐   ☐   ☐   ☐   ☐   ☐   ☐

DATE: ___ / ___ / ___

PROJECT:

FOREMAN:

WEATHER

F° ___   C° ___   ___ AM   ___ PM

HOURS DUE TO BAD WEATHER	ISSUED AND DELAYS

NOTE: ____

COMPLETION DATE	DAYS AHEAD OF SCHEDULE	DAYS BEHIND SCHEDULE

SAFETY AND INCIDENTS

SAFETY ISSUES THAT NEED TO BE ADDRESSED	ACCIDENTS / INCIDENTS / STEPS NEEDED TO RESOLVE

SUMMARY OF THE WORK DONE TODAY

IMPORTANT NOTES

NAME	SIGNATURE

TODAY LABOR

INITIALS	TRADE	START	FINISH	PAID HOURS	OVERTIME	COMPANY
☐ EMPLOYEE ☐ CONTRUCTOR		AM	PM			
☐ EMPLOYEE ☐ CONTRUCTOR		AM	PM			
☐ EMPLOYEE ☐ CONTRUCTOR		AM	PM			
☐ EMPLOYEE ☐ CONTRUCTOR		AM	PM			
☐ EMPLOYEE ☐ CONTRUCTOR		AM	PM			
☐ EMPLOYEE ☐ CONTRUCTOR		AM	PM			
☐ EMPLOYEE ☐ CONTRUCTOR		AM	PM			
☐ EMPLOYEE ☐ CONTRUCTOR		AM	PM			

EQUIPMENT ON SITE	NO. OF UNITE	WORKING YES / NO

HIRED EQUIPMENT	NO. OF UNITE	EQUIPMENT RENTED	FROM	RATE

NAME: _______________________   SIGNATURE: _______________________

MO   TU   WE   TH   FR   SA   SU

☐   ☐   ☐   ☐   ☐   ☐   ☐

DATE: /   /

PROJECT:

FOREMAN:

WEATHER

F° _____ C° _____   _____ AM _____ PM

HOURS DUE TO BAD WEATHER	ISSUED AND DELAYS

NOTE: ____

COMPLETION DATE	DAYS AHEAD OF SCHEDULE	DAYS BEHIND SCHEDULE

SAFETY AND INCIDENTS

SAFETY ISSUES THAT NEED TO BE ADDRESSED	ACCIDENTS / INCIDENTS / STEPS NEEDED TO RESOLVE

SUMMARY OF THE WORK DONE TODAY

IMPORTANT NOTES

NAME	SIGNATURE

TODAY LABOR

INITIALS	TRADE	START	FINISH	PAID HOURS	OVERTIME	COMPANY
☐ EMPLOYEE ☐ CONTRUCTOR		AM	PM			
☐ EMPLOYEE ☐ CONTRUCTOR		AM	PM			
☐ EMPLOYEE ☐ CONTRUCTOR		AM	PM			
☐ EMPLOYEE ☐ CONTRUCTOR		AM	PM			
☐ EMPLOYEE ☐ CONTRUCTOR		AM	PM			
☐ EMPLOYEE ☐ CONTRUCTOR		AM	PM			
☐ EMPLOYEE ☐ CONTRUCTOR		AM	PM			
☐ EMPLOYEE ☐ CONTRUCTOR		AM	PM			

EQUIPMENT ON SITE	NO. OF UNITE	WORKING YES / NO

HIRED EQUIPMENT	NO. OF UNITE	EQUIPMENT RENTED	FROM	RATE

NAME: _______________________   SIGNATURE: _______________________

MO TU WE TH FR SA SU
☐   ☐   ☐   ☐   ☐   ☐   ☐

DATE: ___ / ___ / ___

PROJECT:

FOREMAN:

WEATHER

F° ______   C° ______   ______ AM   ______ PM

HOURS DUE TO BAD WEATHER	ISSUED AND DELAYS

NOTE: ____

COMPLETION DATE	DAYS AHEAD OF SCHEDULE	DAYS BEHIND SCHEDULE

SAFETY AND INCIDENTS

SAFETY ISSUES THAT NEED TO BE ADDRESSED	ACCIDENTS / INCIDENTS / STEPS NEEDED TO RESOLVE

SUMMARY OF THE WORK DONE TODAY

IMPORTANT NOTES

NAME	SIGNATURE

TODAY LABOR

INITIALS	TRADE	START	FINISH	PAID HOURS	OVERTIME	COMPANY
☐ EMPLOYEE ☐ CONTRUCTOR		AM	PM			
☐ EMPLOYEE ☐ CONTRUCTOR		AM	PM			
☐ EMPLOYEE ☐ CONTRUCTOR		AM	PM			
☐ EMPLOYEE ☐ CONTRUCTOR		AM	PM			
☐ EMPLOYEE ☐ CONTRUCTOR		AM	PM			
☐ EMPLOYEE ☐ CONTRUCTOR		AM	PM			
☐ EMPLOYEE ☐ CONTRUCTOR		AM	PM			
☐ EMPLOYEE ☐ CONTRUCTOR		AM	PM			

EQUIPMENT ON SITE	NO. OF UNITE	WORKING YES / NO

HIRED EQUIPMENT	NO. OF UNITE	EQUIPMENT RENTED	FROM	RATE

NAME: ___________________   SIGNATURE: ___________________

MO TU WE TH FR SA SU
☐   ☐   ☐   ☐   ☐   ☐   ☐

DATE: /   /

PROJECT:

FOREMAN:

WEATHER

F°___ C°___   ___ AM ___ PM

HOURS DUE TO BAD WEATHER

ISSUED AND DELAYS

NOTE:

COMPLETION DATE	DAYS AHEAD OF SCHEDULE	DAYS BEHIND SCHEDULE

SAFETY AND INCIDENTS

SAFETY ISSUES THAT NEED TO BE ADDRESSED	ACCIDENTS / INCIDENTS / STEPS NEEDED TO RESOLVE

SUMMARY OF THE WORK DONE TODAY

IMPORTANT NOTES

NAME	SIGNATURE

TODAY LABOR

INITIALS	TRADE	START	FINISH	PAID HOURS	OVERTIME	COMPANY
☐ EMPLOYEE ☐ CONTRUCTOR		AM	PM			
☐ EMPLOYEE ☐ CONTRUCTOR		AM	PM			
☐ EMPLOYEE ☐ CONTRUCTOR		AM	PM			
☐ EMPLOYEE ☐ CONTRUCTOR		AM	PM			
☐ EMPLOYEE ☐ CONTRUCTOR		AM	PM			
☐ EMPLOYEE ☐ CONTRUCTOR		AM	PM			
☐ EMPLOYEE ☐ CONTRUCTOR		AM	PM			
☐ EMPLOYEE ☐ CONTRUCTOR		AM	PM			

EQUIPMENT ON SITE	NO. OF UNITE	WORKING YES / NO

HIRED EQUIPMENT	NO. OF UNITE	EQUIPMENT RENTED	FROM	RATE

NAME: _______________________________   SIGNATURE: _______________________________

| MO | TU | WE | TH | FR | SA | SU |
| ☐ | ☐ | ☐ | ☐ | ☐ | ☐ | ☐ |

DATE: ___ / ___ / ___

PROJECT:

FOREMAN:

WEATHER F° ______ C° ______ ______ AM ______ PM

HOURS DUE TO BAD WEATHER

ISSUED AND DELAYS

NOTE: ____

COMPLETION DATE	DAYS AHEAD OF SCHEDULE	DAYS BEHIND SCHEDULE

SAFETY AND INCIDENTS

SAFETY ISSUES THAT NEED TO BE ADDRESSED	ACCIDENTS / INCIDENTS / STEPS NEEDED TO RESOLVE

SUMMARY OF THE WORK DONE TODAY

IMPORTANT NOTES

NAME	SIGNATURE

TODAY LABOR

INITIALS	TRADE	START	FINISH	PAID HOURS	OVERTIME	COMPANY
☐ EMPLOYEE ☐ CONTRUCTOR		AM	PM			
☐ EMPLOYEE ☐ CONTRUCTOR		AM	PM			
☐ EMPLOYEE ☐ CONTRUCTOR		AM	PM			
☐ EMPLOYEE ☐ CONTRUCTOR		AM	PM			
☐ EMPLOYEE ☐ CONTRUCTOR		AM	PM			
☐ EMPLOYEE ☐ CONTRUCTOR		AM	PM			
☐ EMPLOYEE ☐ CONTRUCTOR		AM	PM			
☐ EMPLOYEE ☐ CONTRUCTOR		AM	PM			

EQUIPMENT ON SITE	NO. OF UNITE	WORKING YES / NO

HIRED EQUIPMENT	NO. OF UNITE	EQUIPMENT RENTED	FROM	RATE

NAME: _______________________   SIGNATURE: _______________________

MO TU WE TH FR SA SU
☐   ☐   ☐   ☐   ☐   ☐   ☐

DATE: /   /

PROJECT:

FOREMAN:

WEATHER

F° _____ C° _____   _____ AM   _____ PM

HOURS DUE TO
BAD WEATHER

ISSUED AND DELAYS

NOTE:

COMPLETION DATE	DAYS AHEAD OF SCHEDULE	DAYS BEHIND SCHEDULE

SAFETY AND INCIDENTS

SAFETY ISSUES THAT NEED TO BE ADDRESSED	ACCIDENTS / INCIDENTS / STEPS NEEDED TO RESOLVE

SUMMARY OF THE WORK DONE TODAY

IMPORTANT NOTES

NAME	SIGNATURE

TODAY LABOR

INITIALS	TRADE	START	FINISH	PAID HOURS	OVERTIME	COMPANY
☐ EMPLOYEE ☐ CONTRUCTOR		AM	PM			
☐ EMPLOYEE ☐ CONTRUCTOR		AM	PM			
☐ EMPLOYEE ☐ CONTRUCTOR		AM	PM			
☐ EMPLOYEE ☐ CONTRUCTOR		AM	PM			
☐ EMPLOYEE ☐ CONTRUCTOR		AM	PM			
☐ EMPLOYEE ☐ CONTRUCTOR		AM	PM			
☐ EMPLOYEE ☐ CONTRUCTOR		AM	PM			
☐ EMPLOYEE ☐ CONTRUCTOR		AM	PM			

EQUIPMENT ON SITE	NO. OF UNITE	WORKING YES / NO

HIRED EQUIPMENT	NO. OF UNITE	EQUIPMENT RENTED	FROM	RATE

NAME: ______________________   SIGNATURE: ______________________

IMPORTANT TELEPHONE NUMBER

▶ NAME __________________________________ PHONE __________________________________
EMAIL ____

▶ NAME __________________________________ PHONE __________________________________
EMAIL ____

▶ NAME __________________________________ PHONE __________________________________
EMAIL ____

▶ NAME __________________________________ PHONE __________________________________
EMAIL ____

▶ NAME __________________________________ PHONE __________________________________
EMAIL ____

▶ NAME __________________________________ PHONE __________________________________
EMAIL ____

▶ NAME __________________________________ PHONE __________________________________
EMAIL ____

▶ NAME __________________________________ PHONE __________________________________
EMAIL ____

▶ NAME __________________________________ PHONE __________________________________
EMAIL ____

▶ NAME __________________________________ PHONE __________________________________
EMAIL ____

▶ NAME __________________________________ PHONE __________________________________
EMAIL ____

▶ NAME __________________________________ PHONE __________________________________
EMAIL ____

▶ NAME __________________________________ PHONE __________________________________
EMAIL ____